THE TWO HARDEST WORDS

A collection of inspirational poems

Rod Ferbrache

AuthorHouse™
1663 Liberty Drive
Bloomington, IN 47403
www.authorhouse.com
Phone: 1-800-839-8640

First published by AuthorHouse   11/3/2010

ISBN: 978-1-4520-7930-1 (sc)

Printed in the United States of America

This book is printed on acid-free paper.

Acknowledgements

This book would never have been printed had it not been for two very dear friends, they know who they are, who so generously funded the production of these poems.

To my daughter Sarah-Jane who was so creative in the design of the cover.

Most of all though, to the Holy Spirit who birthed these verses and allowed me the privilege of being the hand that penned them.

You can see more of my work at www.rodferbrache.com.

The Two Hardest Words

There are words in our language that are hard to pronounce,
There are some which are harder to spell,
And some so familiar they roll off the tongue,
Words that we know so well.
We have words that describe the way that we feel,
To explain just the person we are.
Phrases sum up our opinion of folk,
That express to them that we care.

Descriptions are used to tell of a scene
 That we visited when abroad.
We excitedly tell of a bargain we had
Buying something we could afford.
Then we give reasons of why we did this,
Or our actions caused us to do that.
It might be a jumper we liked the look of,
Or for a wedding we purchased a hat.

Can we remember a day go by
When never a word that we spoke?
Silence for us is unnatural and strange,
For we're generally sociable folk.
Yet sometimes we hear of people we know
Who have fallen out with each other.
It's sometimes between brothers and sisters,
Or worse, between father and mother.

Some words were spoken that cut to the quick,
That once uttered could not be retrieved.
A rift was created, an unbridgeable gap,
At least that's the lie they believed.
Years go by not a word has been spoken,
The distance between them grows.
In fact it is possible so long has time passed,
If you ask, nobody knows
The reason behind the silence,
Why one does not speak to the other.
The matter could so easily be solved,
 But nobody seems to bother.

As I said at the start we have different words,
Some seem so hard to tell.
But it isn't always the length of the words,
Or the fact that we cannot spell.
There comes a time when we refuse to admit
That we are in the wrong.
We only need to speak two words,
Yet it seems to take so long.

You see, those two little words are the two hardest words,
And by some are never spoken,
And because these two words are the two hardest words,
Many relationships remain broken.
What are those two words? The two hardest words?
Do we really need to worry?
Well yes, we do, for those two little words
Are just simply these, "I'm sorry.".

Eagles Wings

"They that wait upon the Lord shall renew their strength. They shall rise up with wings like eagles."

The cliff face stood quite cold and bleak,
With rain splattered moss, bright green.
A windswept ledge was evident,
As yet no sun was seen.
And perched upon this ledge so high,
Pressed hard against its side
Was an eagle resting patiently,
Waiting for a thermal ride.

The lesson learnt when just a chick
Was wait for the sun to rise.
This way the flight is effortless
To rise up in the skies.
It sometimes meant it couldn't go
Just where and when it pleased.
Patience and understanding
Was the key to a life of ease.

For with the sun high in the sky
This bird knew it could soar
Without the need to struggle,
The need to flap no more.
With wings outstretched, unmoving,
The thermals did the work.
It came as second nature,
This waiting had a perk.

The Bible teaches us
In words so plain and true,
If we would know His strength,
Then this we too must do.
To wait, and rest, and keep our eye
Just where the Son turns up.
That way we quickly learn to walk,
Or run, and never drop.

For those who wait upon the Lord
Shall renew their strength each day,
They will not faint or tire
If they let Him have His way.
So if you want to soar like eagles,
The secret is not great.
If the Spirit is not moving you
Then simply wait, and wait

All for our best

If the Lord's eye is on the sparrow, how much more is His eye on me?

It's often we carry our loads of despair,
Worry and tension, sorrows and care.
In control of our problem, no matter how grim,
We fool everybody, we think; how dim.

The Father designed us to give over to Him
Those things which cause fear and reason to sin.
We cannot cope on our own with life,
The temptations and heartaches bring endless strife.

They drag us down like a bag of wet sand,
We feel we can't share it, no one understands.
Destined for nights that are sleepless and long,
Joyless and lonely, left out of the throng.
Yet life must go on, so we grit our teeth
While breaking inside, and crying beneath
The façade of calm, telling folk we can cope,
When the truth of the matter is we've abandoned all hope.

We haven't fooled God, for He sees every heart,
He's numbered each hair, and made every part.
It's He who designed which loads we can bear,
The ones that get heavy He tells us to share.

"Bear each other's burdens," so says the Word.
But we often choose to ignore the Lord.
He says "Because I love you, cast it all on Me,
That's the reason I hung on that rugged rough tree.

So that you don't break under the weight of the load,
But reap your reward at the end of the road."
So if you are struggling with life and its tests,
Remember He works it out all for our best.

Where Two Worlds Met

I love swimming in our lovely outdoor pools; this poem looks back on a couple of days that left a lasting impression on me.

The sun was high up in the sky, the sea was deepest blue.
My heart was set on swimming; in the summer that's what I do.
Every lunchtime off I go to the seaside bathing pool.
I've even gone in winter time when I've oft been called a fool.

This time, however, was different, I saw new people there.
My friends as yet had not arrived, these folk were debonair.
They were sat quite near to me; I could hear them as they spoke.
By clothes and conversation, they were very wealthy folk.

One reached inside his pocket and pulled out a mobile phone.
He very soon was talking in quite a secret tone.
He began by saying about a certain date,
The birthday of his wife was soon so this couldn't be too late.

The present he was buying was not your usual kind,
It was, in fact, a Mercedes Benz that he had planned to find.
£30,000 pounds he said was what he had to spend.
I could tell just by his voice that this was no pretend.

The deal was struck right there and then, the present had been bought.
No mention of a bank loan or neither HP sought.
This was a man of many means and this was just a drop
Of what was at his disposal. He didn't have to stop
And think of how much this had cost him; was the price he paid too high?
But as I sat and listened, the thought that came was "Why?"

The next day came, the scene had changed, gone the man with all his wealth.
A woman came with girl and babe; they all looked poor in health.
The clothes were old and shabby, the people tired and worn.
So different from the previous day where with silver spoon was born.

I heard their conversation 'twas not about a car,
But about the state of benefits that hadn't gone so far.
It was a daily struggle of how to make ends meet.
Not thousands spent on presents, but rather what to eat.

So how the contrasts struck me, of rich and poor sat here.
One consumed by riches, the other gripped by fear.
Two separate worlds had gathered in this same beauty spot.
One where no hardship dwelled, the other not a jot
Of comfort and extravagance, to give to those they love,
This had not gone unnoticed by the Father up above.

He has a heart for widows, for orphans too, He said,
Must all be cared for lovingly, they must be clothed and fed.
To the rich he gave this warning, "Don't store in barns on earth,
But use your money wisely on those things that have true worth."

You cannot take it with you, no room in heaven for gold
That comes from earthly riches, that can't be bought or sold.
So let us spend our time here, aware of needs around.
For those who now sow freely in glory will be crowned.
In heaven there are no rich or poor; in Christ's eyes, all the same.
So let us love them all and bless them in His name.

Faithful God

The rain I thought would never stop, incessantly it poured,
The rain I thought would never stop, incessantly it poured,
Until mid winter came along, then sufficient had been stored.
Our reservoirs were fully stocked, the streams were at full flow,
Restrictions had been lifted, the hosepipe ban could go.
But just how many wondered, stood amazed the rain had come?
How many stopped to thank the Lord for all that He had done?
The rain was sent, but not too much, the earth He did not flood.
His promise had been kept again, He is a Faithful God.

Across the harbour wall I looked, where many folks had gathered.
Predictions had been made that tides would rise above the standard.
The wind was east, the pressure high, as shops made their precautions.
The roads were closed, diversions made, you could almost feel the tension.
But as the hour came and went, the tide began to fall;
How many praised the Lord and on His name did call?
For He has set the boundaries, where He has said, they stood.
His promise had been kept again, He is a Faithful God.

The sky was drawing in the night, as a new sound I heard.
'Twas not the noise of some machine, but the singing of a bird.
To him a season had begun, an urgency it brings
To procreate, to find a mate, that's the reason why it sings.
The evidence is all around, the earth's about to waken.
But does it turn our thoughts to God? Do we find our conscience shaken?
He's formed the seasons one by one, they come in strict rotation.
Yet still the truth evades mankind, to the Creator, not creation
The wonder, joy and praise should go, as flower comes from bud.
Another promise He has kept, He is a Faithful God.

So should we doubt or worry, have anxious thoughts, concerns
If the God we say we worship, tells us "From these lessons learn"?
For if He sends the rain in season, sets a limit on the tide.
If it's Him who wakes the seasons, would we not be better to abide
In the confidence that comes from knowing He will never let us go?
Rather, praise Him for His goodness, let the gratitude within us flow.
I can see that you agree with me, for your head you nod.
Every promise He has kept, He is a Faithful God..

The Lord is a Strong Tower

A Poem taken from Psalm 121.

The city is silent as her people sleep,
No need for a sentry, or a watch to keep.
The gates are now closed, for all is secured,
Each person Is safe and kept by their Lord.
Their Guardian is watchful, He will not sleep,
His presence assures them their rest will be deep.

And as the sky lightens to signal the dawn,
The chill of the night gives way to the morn.
Upon each street strikes the heat of the day,
Yet with His right hand the burning gives way
To the coolest of shade that will cause no hurt,
His protection complete, His eyes always alert.

When the citizens travel in ones or in twos,
Their feet never slip, their way never lose.
They find even in travelling He goes before,
Not only the Pathway but also the door.
It's not for a moment, not e'en for a day,
But both now and forever, today, and always.

And this God of Israel pledges to you
That what He did then, today He'll do too.
He's as watchful as ever, and guards o'er your life,
Protecting, surrounding, in good and in strife.
The sun may burn hot, the moon may wax cold,
Still His right hand upholds you so strong and so bold.

The Keeper of lives, a Covenant Lord,
The One who never goes back on His Word.
As you lift up your eyes to the hills far away,
Be assured of His presence, and in His rest stay

Five happy families

Sunday trading was being debated a number of years ago, and this was a poem I wrote in opposition to the proposal.

Five happy families playing in the park,
The day you see was Sunday, so dad could stay till dark.
The fun they had together was a joy to behold,
But all at once the tears began, for the children had been told
"Dad can't be with you next week, his boss says ' You must work,'
Your mother has to cope alone, so don't drive her berserk."

Four happy families sitting on the beach,
The day you see was Sunday, the tide was just in reach.
The laughter and the pleasure was a joy to behold.
But once again the tears began, 'cause the children had been told,
"Mum won't be with us next week, I'll have to cook the grub,
Her boss has said 'You must work, we're opening up the pub!'"

Three happy families going off to Gran,
The day you see was Sunday, this was their usual plan.
The chatter and embracing was a joy to behold,
But yet again the tears began, as grandmother was told,
"We can't come to you next week, the laws have been relaxed,
Instead you'll have to be alone, our day off has been axed."

Two happy families taking doggie for a walk,
The day you see was Sunday, 'twas always good to talk,
To reminisce and plan, and play, 'twas a joy to behold,
But how the dog began to whine, why wouldn't he be told?
"We can't take you out next week; you'll have to chew your bone,
These walks you love are over, for you its home alone".

One happy family looking rather odd.
The day you see was Sunday, and they're off to worship God.
The singing and the praising was a joy to behold,
Until the tears began to flow, as by the vicar they were told,
"You won't be with me here next week, we'll only meet in heaven,
No day of rest will you enjoy, instead you're working seven!"

It may seem such a tiny wedge, the changing of the law,
But the hammer hitting it will open wide the door,
And once the door is open it will never, ever shut,
The life we all can now enjoy is very soon forgot.

Foolish Things

We have a tortoise that has been my pet for some 48 years. He doesn't do much, he doesn't go far. He spends half the year asleep. Yet when I look at him, I think of that race which the hare had with a tortoise. He was quick to laugh as he ran past at top speed, yet he lived to regret his foolishness.

The Bible speaks about another kind of foolishness, the kind we are encouraged to embrace

God uses the things that are foolish
So often to puzzle the wise,
They think they know all they need to know,
But they're in for such a surprise.
For the things that seem so simple,
So little and lowly and poor,
Are the things that God often uses,
Not those who are proud and tall.
For in God's plan for His Kingdom,
He ordained long ago,
That it's not how great or important you are,
But how close to the Saviour you grow.

To say we believe in a Saviour,
Who died on a tree long ago,
Brings a frown, or a shake of the head, or a laugh,
For to them we really don't know
The things that truly do matter,
The bomb, or famine, or flood.
To them as long as these things exist
There cannot be time for God.
For to believe in Him really is foolish,
To pray, and to fast, and to plead.
They only can see what is on the T.V.
And are blind to their real need.

It appears beyond human logic,
When everything seems to go wrong,
To lift up our eyes, and say "Praise the Lord,"
In order for faith to grow strong.
For people get so discouraged,
When their lives fall into a mess.
Yet we believe what He told us,
That everything works for our best.
For God uses the things that are foolish,
Those things that seem far from good sense,
To bring out the fruit that is sweet to the taste,
In the people the world think are dense.

I thank God that I am foolish,
That to the world what I believe is mad.
I believe in a Saviour, a Lord, a Creator,
Who truly makes me glad.
To be wise as the Bible sees it,
Is to turn our back on those things
That the world would hanker after,
The love that the pop stars sing.

For the love that I know is far richer,
And deeper, which money can't buy.
There's also the promise that says if I trust Him,
I'll live with Him when I die.
So you see, to be laughed at and different,
Is really no hardship at all.
For by being to them so foolish,
I really am wisest of all!

Frustration!

This poem was written following my period of clinical depression, when energy levels were at an all time low. It was with a sense of frustration that this imposed rest was forced upon me.

I looked at the garden and had a thought,
Was a simple brief glimpse of the past.
I remembered the time I could dig at will,
For long periods, satisfactorily fast.
The day, it never seemed long enough
To get all the toils and jobs done.
Rising at dawn, and working straight through
Till the last of the light had gone.
What a sense of achievement was felt
When looking back on the day,
As I got ready to sleep at night
'Twas with contentment on the pillow I lay.

Today as I look at the garden,
With the tasks that lay there undone,
I wonder if somewhere within
Lays the strength to complete just one.
To do it without strain or injury
Is the most one has learnt to hope.
No longer the sense of achievement,
But the knowledge that at least I had coped.
If I lay down at night and sleep
Even that is a blessing to me,
At last I can sink into oblivion,
From the frustration I'm temporarily free.

I remembered the times when I preached the word
With a passion for souls that were lost.
When family worship was churned out each month,
How I lived for these times the most.
I was one of the elders and this I did treasure,
A privilege to be part of the team.
Teaching the children all the new songs,
Seeing them free and so keen.
Each day was a blessing with God by my side,
There was always a song on my mind.
From meeting to meeting, and week to week,
This routine was never a bind.

Today as I think of my witness and walk,
It fails to equal the past.
No longer the desire to study the Word,
Not for me now a day long fast.
Prayer just exists at the start of each day,
Even grace is sometimes missed.
Sharing the Lord with those who are lost
Has been swapped for a 'Things to do list.'
I know in one sense, my doing has stopped,
That being is all I can do.
Yet, what is the point in pretending?
To myself, I have to be true.

The lesson I hope I am learning,
As I'm forced to stop and rest,
Is it's human to want to be active,
That's good, but not necessarily best.
God gives us the strength to tackle each day,
In the way which He appoints.
"My grace is made perfect in weakness,"
He says, and in living by faith He anoints
The little I do compared with before,
When so much was done just for ME!
I needed to come to an end of myself,
If His glory in me folks would see.

Frustration is hard work and exhausting,
It consumes all the peace God would give.
There's a time and a place for grieving the past,
Yet we must move forward and live
The day which the Lord has given to us,
To give what we have, yes, the lot.
Not saying "if only, I wish, why me?"
But appreciate what we have got.
For yeast in the bread makes the whole loaf to rise,
A sprinkling of salt gives food taste.
We can trust the Lord, that what comes our way,
He promises never to waste.

Sitting Alone

When I had a nervous breakdown all that was familiar was swept away. Things looked different, smelled different. A period where it seemed I didn't even know myself; was I becoming a lunatic?

You're sitting alone in your favourite chair,
Enjoying the comfort and light,
Where all that surrounds you is familiar and loved,
The pictures, the décor just right.
It's taken you ages to make it this way,
Much money and time has been spent.
The furniture, carpets, selected by you,
They all even carry your scent.

You feel safe and secure in what is your home,
You know it from ceiling to floor,
The stain on the cushion, the burn on the rug,
Even the chip on the door.
You know it so well that even at night
Your hand can go straight to the switch.
In fact if it fails to light when you want,
The matches are found without hitch.

Because it's familiar you never think twice,
One day it could suddenly end.
You take it for granted the years that have passed
Will go on like a lifelong friend.
Life has a habit of being the same,
It gets so familiar and snug,
Yet by personal experience without giving a clue,
Somebody pulls on the rug.

You're up in the air, then falling back down,
Not knowing at all where you'll land.
When you think you have hit rock bottom at last,
You alas find it's sinking sand!
And then you descend in a place you've not known,
Where all is black and cold.
No switch to be found, no scent that you know,
It's worse than you've ever been told.

Nothing prepares you for this kind of place,
Though advice and knowledge abound!
That's not what you want, and it's not what you need,
It is friends who seem thin on the ground.
In the midst of it all, though it's hard to see,
Is an undeniable trace,
That God has allowed it all in His plan,
In His house it has its place.

It may not be the house that we know,
Nor is it the one we would choose.
But His promise to us is that all of these things
For His glory He's going to use.
I don't always like the 'house' that I'm in,
The rooms are not the ones that I know.
But He leads me along one step at a time,
So by faith not by sight I will go.

Just who would be in Jesus' church?

This was a question that popped into my mind one day when I was working in the garden.

A question slipped into my mind, they often do these days,
Of all the people in our church who walk in different ways.
We've young and old, thin, fat and tall, they vary quite a bit,
But generally are all the same, no matter where they sit.

Respectable and dignified, middle-class, well-spoken too.
We all have cars, lovely homes, and are rather well to do.
Life for most is comfortable with food and drink a-plenty,
We never know of what it's like to sleep outside, cold, empty!

We don't look out of prison with windows barred and bleak,
Where liberty is taken from us with a visit once a week.
No urge to steal for drugs or drink to get us through the day.
No selling of our bodies, not with strangers do we lay.

And so I got to thinking if Jesus had a church,
Who would He have in it, for which people would He search?
Because as I look at Scripture, and see the folk He found,
They were not the sort of people we would like to have around.

Isolated lepers, with sores that smelt and wept,
Tax fiddlers, enemy soldiers were the company He kept.
Rough and rugged fishermen, women of the night,
These were the sort of people we see His heart delight.

So when I ask the question "who would be in Jesus' church?"
The answer that returns to me makes my own heart lurch.
For it would not necessarily be the people here today,
But the ones the world has turned its back on, the ones who stay away.

The reason that they stay away is really plain to see,
They simply don't feel good enough to mix with the likes of me.
There's a feeling of unworthiness that can keep them from this place,
Their shame and degradation, isolation and disgrace.

Yet Jesus always had the time, in fact He sought them out.
Never did He turn away, never did He doubt
That in the schemes of glory there would be a place
For the dirty, down and out; He made for them a space.

So as we go to church each week, and fill the same old seat,
If we see a stranger, let's stand and go to greet
Those people Jesus sends us, don't make them feel alone,
For it was always His intention this should be their home.

Lord Make me a Blessing

This was the first poem that I wrote over 25 years ago.
We never know what influence we have on people's lives, and may not fully know until we reach eternity.
May it be a challenge to us all that if we want to be a blessing it has to be on His terms not ours.

Lord make me a blessing in all I do and say,
Lord make me a blessing in all I do and say,
I want to be what You were as You walked the narrow way.
For everywhere You went in every love-filled day,
You touched and healed, and helped each one that in Your presence stayed.
Lord You were a blessing to the woman at the well,
To Your disciple Peter who before Your trial fell.
To the lepers who were outcasts, to the beggars and the lame,
Lord You were a blessing, please make me the same.

Lord make me a blessing especially in my home,
But send me only nice folk to share my jam and scone.
For Lord I'd really be put out if at my door there came
A dirty, smelly, long-haired lout who stood there in his shame.
Lord make me a blessing to everyone I meet,
While I do my shopping and I'm walking in the street.
But Lord You really can't expect for me to help that drunk
Who's fallen off his seat and in the gutter sunk.
He's there a victim of himself, there's no-one else to blame,
But Lord, make me a blessing, as I go out in Your Name.

Lord make me a blessing as I go up to my school,
I would be a light for You, and there I'd be a fool.
But Lord don't ask that I should speak about my life in You,
Nor ask me turn the other cheek, or leave revenge to You.
To do that is too hard Lord, that's just not playing the game,
But Lord make me a blessing at school just the same.
Lord make me a blessing as I go about my work,
To those You put into my path may Lord I never shirk,
Just let me work with Christians, where we all believe the same.
Yet Lord, make me a blessing, as I speak out in Your name.

Lord make me a blessing in all I do and say.
I want to be what You were as You walked the narrow way.
I want to be a blessing in my work, home, school and walk,
But Lord my prayer so often is a lot of empty talk.
"My children, if a blessing to me you want to be,
Count not the cost or loss of face if Christ your friends would see,
Because My walk is lonely, My cross so hard to bear,
And few there are who wish to be a blessing where
I would lead, and say just when and what to say.
Or who to see, and help, and share the burdens of their day.
I ask of you just one thing, and that is when you pray
Lord make me a blessing, say "Master, I obey."

The School Bully

My days at school were not particularly happy ones. In fact I couldn't wait to leave.
This was mainly due to bullying. Fifteen years ago I had the chance to get even; this is what the poem is about.

There once was a boy who was frightened of school,
The thought of it filled him with dread.
For 'twas many a time he said he was ill,
And often spent days tucked in bed.

You see, there were boys who bullied and punched,
They roamed the playground in gangs,
Threatening, taunting, fearsome they were,
Even lying in wait in the lanes.

So schooling was wasted, so little achieved,
"Could do better than this," his reports read.
The potential was there, if only applied,
But too often alone, stuck in bed.

The years soon passed by and a job was found,
Then in time moved on to another.
From growing to gardening, from bakery to post,
New skills were learnt without bother.

School memories faded, along with the hurt,
The family quickly did grow.
He little expected the time would come
When he'd come face to face with his foe.

The bully was seeking work for himself,
Some thirty odd years had gone by.
Yet when the victim set eyes on this man
He realised the hurt had not died.

Yet strange how the tables had turned around,
Revenge was an option, a choice.
The one who was bullied, helpless and dumb,
Was a person who now had a voice.

Do I get my own back on this villain of old?
Shall I get even with him and be done?
Yet sensed if he gave in to a feeling like this,
It wouldn't be him who had won.

He felt the Lord say quite clearly to him
"Forgiveness is surely the way".
So the hurt he surrendered, the past put behind,
And a victory was won that day.

You see, I was that boy, and I am that man,
Thanks to His power I could forgive.
'Twas His compassion that reached out that day,
As my motives I allowed Him to sieve.

Many experiences have I known,
Bereavement, anguish and pain.
None of these could I face in my strength,
But had to call on His name.

There are things in our lives which are hard to face,
We bury them deep in our soul.
But the Lord's desire is to draw them out,
So our lives can be healthy and whole.

We can't treat ourselves, we haven't the means.
Let's learn to acknowledge this fact.
It's not always for us to sort things out;
We must give God permission to act.

Friends

The older you get the more you learn to value your friends. True friends know you at your worst and yet still want to know you. They may only be counted on one hand, but each one enriches our lives beyond measure.

There aren't many things in life that are fun,
That are great to do on your own.
We all need friends to play with at school,
You can't speak to yourself on the phone.
Stamps can't swap themselves, you need friends
Who will give the ones that you still need to get.
A day on the beach with only yourself
Is so dull, you'll not even get wet.

In the playground alone, with bullies you dread,
And your heart is pounding with fear,
That's the time when you value the friend that you have,
That's the time when you need someone near.
If you've heard a great joke and had a good laugh
There needs to be someone to tell,
If you're lying in bed with mumps or the flu,
It helps when they say, "Please get well!"

When you get older and life knocks you about,
And sorrow abounds in good measure,
It's then that it matters you've kept in touch
With those friendships that you really treasure.
You see, a true friend is one who is there
In joy, in pain, and in sorrow.
They were there yesterday, they are with you today,
And for certain will be there tomorrow.

The greatest example of friendship we have,
Is shown in the life of our Saviour.
With Him is no changing of feelings and moods,
No demands that we owe Him a favour.
His love is the same regardless of us,
It varies not day from day.
All that He asks is we love Him back too,
Then forever within us He'll stay.

Fallen Leaves

This poem came about following an unseasonal gale during the night, at the beginning of May, a couple of years ago. It was a heart-rending sight going into work the following day to see so many young fresh leaves lying in the gutter. So much potential that had come to nothing.

The winter is always so wet and dark,
With days that are long and bleak.
Everything seems so dead and bare
That some comfort we have to seek.
We look for the sign that marks the turn
Of the sun on its southward track,
That glimmer of light at 5 o'clock
Means that spring will soon be back.

The first shoots of life emerge from the trees,
Then the daffodils burst into bloom.
At just the same time the willow's flower comes,
It means that the rest will come soon.
The swallows arrive and the dawn chorus sings,
There is now so much to see.
April has gone, and May has arrived,
With leaves covering every tree.

But up came the wind, it blew through the night,
By morning 'twas plain to all,
That due to the force of the wind and the rain,
Those lovely young leaves did fall.
The roads and gutters were strewn with debris,
With leaves that barely were born.
So filled with potential to cool and to shade,
Now cast down, looking so forlorn.

Their purpose cut short by the force of the storm,
Till autumn they were destined to dress
The branches that birthed them and held them in place,
Now their absence brought instant distress.
The beauty, the promise, the order,
In fact, the season we had come to expect,
Had come to an end that was premature;
There they were, fallen and wrecked!

I'm sure you know of folks – I certainly do,
That walked with the Lord when quite young.
The Word formed a major part of their life,
From outside they looked so strong.
But a storm came along and blew them about,
Until shortly thereafter they fell.
The road of life is strewn with such folk,
What a lesson their lives do tell.

They were full of potential, God was so real,
You looked at them feeling so sure
That nothing could shake the faith that they had,
There was nothing they couldn't endure.
Yet somehow the enemy got in and worked,
To cause doubt and confusion to rise.
The bait was taken, the loved one soon fell,
And blindness enveloped their eyes.

Have we given up hope, feeling despair?
Do we think they could never return?
Have they wandered too far, are they out of sight?
Does the hurt in our heart ever burn?
Remember the prodigal son who left all,
He squandered his life for a time,
Yet with money all gone and hungry,
For home he began to pine.

As I look at the trees with a year gone by,
There are leaves once again on the branch.
New life has emerged, the past is forgotten,
 It's as if there's a second chance.
We must not lose hope for the loved one who fell,
Let us pray them back to the place
Where forgiveness flows, acceptance is found,
Where God pours out His mercy and grace.

He as a Father is out on the road;
He scans the horizon to see
The broken and contrite sinner return,
The one He had to watch flee.
The arms are stretched wide, can you see His tears flow?
His heart, did you hear, skip a beat?
There they are, they're on the way back.
The Father, He runs out to greet.

He didn't give up and neither should we,
Let us claim them again for His crown.
We'll continue to hold them in the arms of faith,
'Til the final sunset goes down.
Have you a loved one who has wandered away?
Do you grieve, have you shed many tears?
Then give them to Jesus, He died for each one,
And He can restore the years
The locusts have eaten, those times of waste,
He can use everything we thought lost.
So trust Him and claim them, they're precious, each one.
That's why Jesus paid such a cost.

Rain

It's in every conversation that we seem to have each day,
We have to comment on it no matter what we say.
There are sayings all about it; we blame it for our ills.
Sometimes it makes us boiling hot and other times it chills.
We chat about the weather, often at great length,
The rain, the sun, the cold and wet, plus measure the wind strength.

One of my favourite memories when the children were quite small,
We'd often take them camping and we always had a ball.
Living in a six-berth tent with just room to swing a cat,
The sound of rain on canvas, a gentle pitter-pat.
We even felt quite comfy when wind blew and rain lashed down.
Of course, if it went on too long then the kids did start to frown.

We often seem too quick to moan about a spot of rain,
With washing out, or holiday, it can be quite a pain.
But think again how long we would last if rain were to never drop,
If when we turned the tap on, the flow at once would stop.
For we rely on water to do so many things,
Without a second thought we hear the kettle sing.

Yet isn't rain a miracle the way it falls down from the sky
And brings new life upon the earth that previously was dry,
And then it runs into the sea and there gets mixed with salt,
Then it's caught back up again, the process doesn't halt.
It's just the same with God our Father, His blessings freely give,
We can keep them flowing outward simply by the way we live.

Snow

It's in every conversation that we seem to have each day,
We have to comment on it no matter what we say.
There are sayings all about it; we blame it for our ills,
Sometimes it makes us boiling hot and other times it chills.
We chat about the weather, often at great length,
The rain, the sun, the cold and wet, and measure the wind strength.

Even though I'm adult, excitement starts to rise
When snow and ice are forecast, I eagerly scan the skies.
This year was quite a good one, for the lovely white, cold stuff,
The only one regret I had was there wasn't quite enough.
It only stayed a day or two, and in no time all was gone.
Because it was a work day I couldn't have much fun.

I did take lots of photos for a memory of the day,
Everything looked so different, oh why could it not stay?
A few more days, perhaps a week, it really wouldn't hurt,
But no, it soon began to disappear and left a load of dirt.

Yet every snowflake's different, it's so hard to take it in,
How can each one vary? Where does one begin
To try and understand it, to reason, fathom out.
It tells me of a great Creator, I really have no doubt.

And if He takes such trouble with every single flake,
Then let me tell each one of you there can be no mistake.
You are not here by accident, a random act of fate.
God has a plan for each of us…look to Him, it's not too late.

Wind

It's in every conversation that we seem to have each day,
We have to comment on it no matter what we say.
There are sayings all about it; we blame it for our ills,
Sometimes it makes us boiling hot and other times it chills.
We chat about the weather, often at great length,
The rain, the sun, the cold and wet, and measure the wind strength.

This time we look at something that you cannot see or taste.
You cannot reach and touch it, nor can you smell or waste.
Yet it's something all around us, it can vary quite a lot.
Man has tried to harness it to generate some watts.

Of course it's wind we're thinking of, we feel it every day.
And if you are a cyclist it can really make you sway.

There's lots we can do with it, fly kites, build windmills and sail.
But all of these are useless when the winds are light, or fail.

And yet we saw the power that the wind could bring to bear,
When the hurricane struck us, then it was a thing to fear.
But we're fascinated by its strength and I need to know each day
By looking at the weather vane, which would be a sheltered bay.
Or when to light a bonfire to keep the neighbours sweet,
We're grateful for a gentle breeze to soothe us in the heat.

We can't touch God, or taste Him; we can't see Him with our eye,
Yet like the wind we feel around us, we can know Him if we try.
For He is all around us, with faith His presence know.
His purposes are revealed to us, He simply says "let go."

Sunshine

It's in every conversation that we seem to have each day,
We have to comment on it no matter what we say.
There are sayings all about it; we blame it for our ills.
Sometimes it makes us boiling hot and other times it chills.
We chat about the weather, often at great length,
The rain, the sun, the cold and wet, and measure the wind strength.

I've kept the best till last; I think that you'll agree
That out of all the features, it's this one we like to see.
Its presence cheers the heart for sure; on our face it puts a smile,
It's great for sitting out in, at least for a short while.
We all feel better for it, when we've had a bit of sun,
I'm always saddened when the time that summer's come and gone.

Again I see a miracle each time I see this star,
Not just for the warmth it gives us, but when I consider just how far
It is away from us and yet its presence feel,
If no sun would ever shine again we'd all be cold as steel.
Yes, too far away and we would freeze, too close and we would fry,
Yet where it is, it's so precise, way up in the sky.

It isn't just coincidence the place that it is found,
Such measurement is so exact the figures do astound.
It's so much bigger than the moon, the distance greater too,
Yet there are times just now and then it can be hid from view.
Do you remember the eclipse? 'Twas awesome don't you think?
Yet greater far the One who made it, I hope you see the link.

Thunder

It's in every conversation that we seem to have each day,
We have to comment on it no matter what we say.
There are sayings all about it, we blame it for our ills.
Sometimes it makes us boiling hot and other times it chills.
We chat about the weather, often at great length,
The rain, the sun, the cold and wet, and measure the wind strength.

I love extremes of weather, of record-breaking stuff,
Both hot and coldest temperatures and enjoy the sea when rough.
But the ultimate experience, at least the one I like the best,
Is the noisiest spectacular that puts the bravest to the test.
I mean of course a thunderstorm, where skies light with every flash,
And animals cower in corners at the sound of every crash.

Such a display of power is hard to comprehend,
How something so enormous can such energy expend.
We are told a flash of lightening can a city energise,
Yet often comes so suddenly, we are caught out in surprise.

I love to gaze up heavenward and marvel at this show,
It tells me of a mighty God, someone so vast to know.
The sound of it is awesome, it shakes the house I'm in,
You simply can't ignore it, it's making such a din.
Yet in the midst of all the power one fact I can't dismiss,
Is in the greatness of its Maker, He is mine and I am His.

Sunset

I wrote this poem during the conflict in Serbia when people had to venture out at night to get water in fear of snipers.

Tonight I watched the sun go down, in shades of burning red,
The day had ended as it came with all the island fed.
And as I walked along the road the lights in homes came on,
Within the windows as I passed, sat people labours done.

To them it was a normal day, no tragedy or fear
Had knocked upon their door, no mortars falling near.
Bird song and the high-pitched cheep of grasshopper was heard,
Not by the sound of weeping was the evening stillness stirred.

A bed for them was waiting, which would surely give them rest,
Not bloodstained by a victim with shrapnel in their chest.
They drank their cup of coffee with water that was clean.
Not from a dried up river where snipers could be seen.

To them the sound of shooting was a million miles away,
For them there just had ended another normal day.
But as I watched the sun go down, the truth just dawned on me;
Another day had started for a people not so free.

The things we take for granted, we look on as our right,
For them a daily battle which silently they fight.
For them no singing of a bird, no opening of a flower,
But a never-ending nightmare as they struggle for the power -

live their lives the way we do, to travel just at will,
To eat a meal in such a way that all may have their fill.
The life they seek for children, who never yet have played,
Is something so elusive, it's yet to be displayed.
The world can look so different depending where you live,
The sunset can be beauty depending where you live.

Tears ...The Souls rain

It says in Psalm 34 "The Lord is close to the broken-hearted and saves those who are crushed in spirit."
Therefore none of our tears are wasted or overlooked.

The young married couple had dreamt of the day
When a daughter or son would be born.
At last the time came for the wife to give birth
Though the labour was long, and she worn.
Nothing could stop the joy in their hearts,
As she held the young babe to her breast.
A tear trickled down the young father's cheek,
As he looked at the infant at rest.
So innocent there, untouched by the world,
With a peace that nothing could shake.
He was choked with emotion, full of pride too,
That he felt his heart would break.

The child quickly grew, and to school she did go,
Her lessons she learnt with ease.
A good sense of humour, well-liked in the class,
A person who loved a good tease.
In no time at all university loomed,
With all of the study that meant.
She excelled in her work, a degree was attained,
A career in medicine spent.
As her parents watched on graduation day
Their daughter walk forward so meek,
Their eyes filled with water, a lump in their throats,
And tears trickled down both their cheeks.

One day she arrived at the family home,
With a young man they never had seen.
"I'd like you to meet my husband to be,"
She said in a voice so keen.
Dad looked at Mum, Mum spluttered out loud,
"We really had no idea."
"Oh mummy, we're headlong in love, can't you see?
You really have nothing to fear!"
The church was arranged, the outfits were bought,
The wedding day quickly arrived.
What a picture she made, their own little girl
Was now someone else's bride.
Once again they felt that tear trickling down,
As they let their daughter go.
On the way home, it struck them so hard,
The trickle turned into a flow.

The parents had brought up their girl in the Lord,
She walked with Him close to her side.
But with pressures of family, career, and time,
She gradually started to slide.
At first, wasn't much, just her prayer time got dropped
In an effort to fit it all in.
But before very long, she was staying out late,
And then a young man led her to sin.
How it broke the hearts of her parents close by,
As they saw all their dreams disappear.
It wasn't for joy, nor pleasure, or pride
That they ended up shedding a tear.

Like the Prodigal son in the story of old,
'Twas only when nothing remained
She came to her senses, returned to her home.
Begged forgiveness from those she had pained.
There were tears shed that night, for the lost had been found,
They were gripped in a tight embrace.
It mattered not what the neighbours had thought,
Or to the family, had brought disgrace.
Their child was back home, to the ones who had loved
Throughout this crisis and pain.
Tears were a symbol of the compassion they felt,
But their faces expressed all the strain.

Tears are the rain that waters the soul,
As it passes through seasons which change.
Some filled with such joy, inexpressibly good,
The thought of sorrow seems strange.
But all of us know from personal expense,
That grief comes to each one in turn.
Whether it be the loss of a son,
Or a difficult lesson to learn.
Perhaps it's our way of coping with pain,

Or in compassion, or being a friend.
It never hurts to show that we care,
If a few tears on our loved ones we spend.

When Lazarus died, and Jesus was told
His friend had passed away,
He didn't pretend He was under control,
Or even call it a day.
He came to Bethany, to the home that He loved,
To the place He had eaten and slept.
It wasn't the words that He spoke that day
We remember just that, "He wept."
He cried tears of sadness, just as we do,
There were times of passion He felt.
Remember that night in the garden alone,
There fell sweat-drops of blood where He knelt.

The tears that you shed in secret,
The emotions that run so deep,
He sees every drop, He knows every heart,
And near to His side He will keep
Those who are hurting, confused, at an end.
He promises always to stay
Until the time comes, as He says in His Word,
"All tears will be wiped away."

The Clematis and the Oak

The Gardener stood with his hand outstretched and in it held a seed,
A closer look revealed to me it wasn't any weed.
For in his grasp I clearly saw an acorn small and round,
I wondered for a moment the reason why he found
The need to have this item so common, so well-known,
But he said to me, you wait and see, until it's fully grown.

Into the ground the acorn went, 'twas tended with such care,
Yet what seemed to me like endless months, the soil remained so bare.
But then one day I saw a shoot emerge above the soil,
The Gardener too had noticed it, but never ceased to toil.
He weeded, feeded, kept an eye on what was now an oak.
The ground around was kept so clean, this seedling mustn't choke.

And then he stretched his hand again; I leant forward so I could see,
The tiny seed inside his grasp was as small as small could be.
He told me this was a special seed that needed extra care,
It couldn't go into open ground that now was cold and bare.
It went inside the glasshouse where conditions were just right,
The Gardener gave it water and gave it heat and light.

It too began to germinate into a plant so fair,
Eventually it too was placed outside in the fresh air.
The years went by unnoticed, the oak and plant grew well,
The tree rose tall and handsome, the clematis, such a sweet smell.
But something happened gradually, that no-one seemed to see,
The plant and tree grew bit by bit until it came to be
The plant reached out and grasped the oak and both grew up together,
They soon became inseparable, that no matter what the weather
The oak gave to the plant support and strength against the weather,
The plant brought scent and beauty as they wrapped around each other.

I met the Gardener recently; we spoke of this and that,
It didn't take so very long before we began to chat
About the tree before us, and the beauty of the shrub.
I pointed out those two were one, and what an awful job
That we would have to separate, the two now joined together.
He said that wasn't in the plan, and had I thought that whether
When he had planted both those seeds he had upon his mind,
That if he grew them close enough together they would bind.

Marriage brings so many strengths; there are challenges with it too,
But as you start this step together there's one thing that you must do,
And that is like our story of the oak tree and the flower,
If you hold each other tightly you will have such power.
Let God who brought you both together, who tends both plants and earth
Give you both a marriage that you agree is worth
More than any money, than any life apart.
I urge you both, that every day you give your life, your heart
To one another, may you both to each be ever true.
Start and end each day together, with the words "I do love you".

Lord, when did You Know?

As You brought into being this world of ours,
The seas and the earth, birds, animals, flowers,
How far did You look down the road of time?
When you fashioned each leaf of the very first vine.
What did You think as the stars shone above?
Was the moon created simply for love?
And did the sun shine just to give off its heat?
Is the reason for animals just for their meat?
Things didn't evolve; they were part of a plan,
Right there in Genesis, the redemption of man.

When You made that first tree did Your eye shed a tear?
Did You see the time when Your Son would hang there?
Were You tempted to make the bark of soft wood
To ease His pain just as a father would?

As You added the thorns to the desert bush,
Did You think of the time the soldiers would push
Them into the brow of Your precious Son?
Did You ever regret just what You had done?
When You laid the foundations with iron ore
Could You see the nails, which in His hands tore?
Was it painful to You? Could Your tender heart feel
The stab of the spear with its tip of steel?

At the beginning of time when You made all these things,
Did You stop to consider the pain it would bring?
Why was man made, if You knew he would slay
The dear Son of God, some dark evil day.
As You fashioned each stone as though it was hewn,
When did You realise it was for a tomb?
When You planted that garden for man to dwell,
Did You think of Gethsemane, and the road to Hell
That Jesus would enter to take my place,
To carry my shame, to bear my disgrace?

For You gave the thorns, the nails and the tree,
And left them with man knowing how they would be
Used as instruments to kill Your dear Son.
But yet, as I ponder it, Your will was done.
You loved us completely, You could not forego
The work of creation if You, we would know.

I can't understand such love, so great.
A love so much greater than a world full of hate.
A Creator who saw before time began,
Exactly the way the gulf to span
Between Him and I, the gain, the loss,
For without a tree there could be no Cross.
Without a Cross, no forgiveness of sin,
But because of the Cross, I have Him within.

The Countdown to Christmas

'Twas towards the end of August,
When I saw the first Christmas card.
I had come from the beach, the sun was quite hot,
Every thought of that season was barred.
I was hanging my bathers and towel on the line,
I was hoping overnight they would dry,
"I won't be forced at this time of year
To think of Christmas" I cried.

September came next and it brought no great shock,
When I opened the paper and read,
Page upon page of menus and facts,
Of where you can go and be fed.
There are luncheons and buffets, dinner and dance,
Black tie was an option too,
If you don't book now, come Christmas Day,
You can only look forward to stew!

Before we knew it October was here,
The leaves on the trees start to fall,
But down at the village a man was out,
Climbing a ladder so tall.
There were lights to erect, Santa and sleigh,
Even the nativity scene.
In October I thought what a sad state he's in,
The haste seemed a little obscene.

Bonfire night came, with its pops and its bangs,
People setting fire to their cash.
I thought to myself late night opening is next,
It will be here in just a flash.
So how many days before Christmas are left?
How much have you got to do
Before the big day arrives as it will,
I guess there are still quite a few?

Let's all get depressed as I read out the list,
Of what still lies ahead.
If you get all this done by Christmas day,
You'll only be fit for bed.
There's still the odd card that has to be sent,
The presents are still to wrap.
Tree lights are playing up again,
And my nerves are ready to snap.

I won't bother with crackers, they weren't that great,
They all looked a little bit flat,
Gran can't get the jokes and she jumps when they crack,
And mum looks so daft in her hat.
I must order the cream and double the milk,
I'll probably do one more shop.
When Christmas day comes and the family arrives,
I'll only be fit to drop.

We make all our lists, fulfill all our tasks,
And do so much to prepare
For this annual event that leaps from the page,
I wonder if we would dare
Put all this aside and spend time instead,
Preparing ourselves for the One,
Who gave us Christmas, this season we love,
And the gift of His dear Son.

He too had a list of things on His mind,
He knew He had to get done,
There was so much to plan and make ready,
Before Jesus Christ could come.
A willing couple had to be found,
Someone who wouldn't shirk.
Simply being obedient, humble and true,
If the plan of salvation would work.

A star had to be made, that at just the right time,
Would lead the kings to the child.
The heavenly choir was summoned to sing,
To the shepherds who on the hills toiled.
If you look in the Bible and see God's plan,
You'll find it went back many years.
All during that time, God was at work,
To take away all our fears.
You see Christ is not just for Christmas,
He must be in all that we do,
I've found that He's made such a difference,
Today – I ask, how about you?

Christmas Was Never Like This!

How different this Christmas from the first long ago,
No cards, food and parties, lights, snow, mistletoe.
There were no lists of presents, which have to be bought.
The biggest and best tree did not need to be sought.

No hustle and bustle, no stress and tension,
To think, of the turkey, there was never a mention.
No crackers, no pudding, and no Santa Claus,
No drinking and dancing that goes on without pause.

No stocking hung bulging at the foot of the bed,
Nor the sending of greetings, either spoken or read.
The very first Christmas had no laden table,
Just a girl and a man in a smelly, cold stable.

She, scared of the future, he loyal and true,
Both made aware of the child that was due.
No fairy lights twinkle, just a solitary star,
No family around them, only men from afar.

The Child born to be King, yet without a throne,
In a place of hostility, not in His own home.
Yet He came and brought peace, hope, love and great joy.
How much we do owe to the birth of this boy?

I know that first Christmas was never like this,
Yet with Him as your Saviour you will never need miss
The true meaning of Christmas, His peace and His joy,
For He's now King of Kings, no longer a boy.

Bring the Christ back to Christmas, it's where He belongs,
That's the reason we gather, why we sing all these songs.
If your life lacks true meaning, look no further than here,
Make welcome this Christmas, the Lord Jesus so dear.

The Changing Scenes of Christmas

Christmas has changed don't you think
From the ones when I was a lad?
Those times were special, simple and good,
Just my brothers and me, Mum and Dad.
The ceiling was covered in paper chains,
There was holly and ivy – no tree,
Dad found a branch of evergreen oak,
Was as good as the real thing to me.

We'd go to bed early on Christmas Eve,
Made the night go quicker we thought,
But every so often I'd creep down the bed,
To feel what Santa had brought.
One of Dad's socks did the trick every year,
Was amazing how much it would stretch,
We'd jump in their bed at the crack of dawn,
And our stockings we'd one by one fetch.

Christmas has changed don't you think,
From the ones when I was a teen?
There were all sorts of decisions to make,
Like where to spend Christmas – I mean
Should I go to my girlfriend's house?
Or should she come over to us?
What a difficult job to please everyone,
Yet we managed without too much fuss.

I remember one year on Boxing Day,
The party was held at my Gran,
It had snowed overnight but the roads were clear,
To drive Judy home was the plan.
But as evening fell so did the snow
'Twas too deep to drive into town,
So she came home with me, and much to my glee,
From my parents not even a frown.

Christmas has changed don't you think,
From the time when my children were small?
There were wish lists and hints dropped,
And the hope was that Santa would call.
It was their turn to jump on our bed in the dark,
"Can we get up, is it time?"
No matter that Dad had worked a hundred-hour week,
"Oh please can we get up?" they'd whine.

I loved Boxing Day; we'd play with their toys,
There was always something to make.
Lego was great; we'd build something big,
Like airports and towns with a lake.
My Little Pony, the Care Bears and Flumps,
Sylvanian families were fun,
The hours we spent on the floor with these things,
Just to think makes my throat grow a lump.

Christmas has changed don't you think,
From that first Christmas long ago?
But has it, or is it the things we have done,
That has caused the occasion to grow?
We still celebrate the King who was born
In a stable so cold and bare.
We sing of the Wise Men, who came from so far,
To worship, and give, and stare
Into the eyes of the Christ-child so small,
A child who was destined to die,
We still praise His name and trust in His cross,
That was given for you and for I.

The story of Christmas remains the same;
The response is for us to give.
We either accept or reject this gift,
We can choose to die or to live.
Christmas can change from the one that you know,
The one that is never the same,
Just come to the Saviour, He beckons to you,
Listen, He's calling your name

Valleys and Mountains

In life it's not long ere you discover
There are mountains and valleys and hills.
The going is seldom on even ground,
But a struggle with feelings and wills.
We long for a time when things level out,
And the mountains reduce to a plain,
Or the summit is reached and the climb is behind,
Along with the tears and the pain.

Yet the Lord says "Look not to the mountain,
For it's awesome, frightening and bare.
Turn your eyes up to Me; I'm greater you'll see,
Than the obstacle standing there.
My promise to you is not for a walk
Which is easy and smooth and wide,
But the path that you take is narrow and steep,
With room just for Me by your side.

Yet we travel that path together,
For I am the guide of your life.
And the hope that we share, is when we reach there
No more will you know such strife.
Don't be dismayed by the valleys,
With sides that are dark and steep.
Don't be concerned and feel all hemmed in,
For haven't I promised to keep
Your footsteps beside still waters,
Your eyes on pastures green,
For on mountaintops high, which reach to the sky,
Such plenty is never seen.

For a valley is always a place where you grow,
Life is evident, fresh and new.
It's a place that is watered by springs and rain,
And the daily anointing of dew.
The valley's a place of protection,
Sheltered from wind and storm.
A place of shade and shadow,
Yet I stay just to keep you warm.
It's not a place to be dreaded,
Or a depth, which you don't want to go,
For the food is sweet, if you stop to eat,

And My Presence you'll surely know".

Contents

Lightning Source UK Ltd.
Milton Keynes UK
UKIC01n0925300414
230810UK00001B/5